A *of* Expectations

Selected poems

by

Jens Fink-Jensen

ISBN: 978-81-8253-945-7
First Edition: 2022
Rs. 200/-

Cyberwit.net
HIG 45 Kaushambi Kunj, Kalindipuram
Allahabad - 211011 (U.P.) India
http://www.cyberwit.net
Tel: +(91) 9415091004
E-mail: info@cyberwit.net

Printed at Repro India Limited.

Contents

World in an Eye

Colours in Between

1

I listen
completely quiet in the night
when the winds betray the darkness

I hug
the arms of the trees
swishing competitively

I walk
between the walls of the houses
as they cast shadows for the sunbeams

I am silent
like a stone Like a mountain
when the world begins to fall ...

2

The city white The streets white
Boats of the dreams on the lake Mirrors and swans
Waves ...

We meet Talk in the green
Do not hear each other in the sea:
Blue blue

Everything is in quiet motion Eyes
meet and part and divide
Yellow teeth ...

The children dashing about Boats on their way out
The houses and the water with the colours:
Black black hands

3

Processions of the streets
Come to meet us
Their cloaks dim the light

I try to hold us back
while they disperse in the alleys
We need eyes like them!

And we don't know at all
who they are
Only that they're searching for us:

The light meets us dimly
but we do not understand their language
We don't have the maps they have

4

There is no summer in this city
I know its extent Its ways
Ways out in case of unwanted meetings

I am no city Perhaps a budding
summer Perhaps I contain opportunities
for lots of unwanted encounters But

I do not want ... Not summer if
it slips away soon after anyway Look
the desert in the eye Stabilising and spreading ...

But that's not who we are. We travel
so far within ourselves And without
that we never need seasons

5

Most of all we are humans
with their different languages and boundaries
and who dare not speak to and touch each other

We with our fear of wars of prisons
of torture of strangers of the night
Night sneakers Obvious idiots in daytime

We have our own songs
We take our own steps across borders
We have plenty of life to exchange

We have many wars yet to come
With our blood of the future we acknowledge
that we still owe the most smiles

6

As soon as the pictures are taken
the soldiers set out for the battlefields
in the uniforms we bought for them

I dip my gaze in world wine
but I do not see any clearer Not before
someone else manages to catch it

and I can look all the way to
the other side of myself
on the white backs of the pictures

When the light is completely out
we follow the armies out of the forest
into their dreams Away from ourselves

7

It takes silence to escape
We must be so quiet that we can't
hear ourselves Only trust ourselves

The thoughts we send ahead
we seal with our dictating mouths
The songs must not be sung yet

Who held us in captivity
Other than ourselves
we ask panting

We are on our way I think The thoughts
are waiting for us Those we hide away
when anxiety comes back

8

Still in the tower I remember A man
and a woman and a small black child
All black with the light behind them

Coming into the tower where I am
Completely quiet as if they have been here before
I don't think they know my stone

I'm also completely quiet My own power
is not big enough to
meet them Now I see the real colours

Completely white faces They don't believe anything
can last this long Be this cold This warm
of longing for just a small exchange of words

9

I am part of the refractions of light
I'm the needle eye of black and white
My skin is covered by the travels of colours:

The differences between us The differences in us
Our ability to see changes in the level
When our eyes teach us to save our lives

And there is no one Not even myself
who will call these colours real
even if they are needed in order to live

But they are also the saddest colours
And although they are necessary and reassuring
They gleam of betrayal

10

I will not ask you anything Not
ask anyone anything Only
eat the fruits as if no one saw it

Which fruits you will ask Never mind
I will answer It is your silence Your
lies I want to get rid of The fruits of them

Infatuations of spring Caresses of summer
Autumn's tenderness Winter's aching
pictures Their white snowy births

When we are quiet and have forgotten the stars
and rediscover them Wars are approaching:
Other stars have better planets!

11

Whispers tell lies They say
But that's not true I say
It's the truth we aren't allowed to hear

Why may I not tell you
that I love you Why should I
whisper it into a cold night's ears?

We need to step up the sounds
step up the colours Step up each other
Let's show how strong we are

Nature that we have bossed about
waits with its inarticulate wounds
for us to make peace

12

There is a world Singing waves of
hope No continents without hunger
Created and planned by people who have enough to eat

These masters Ruling exhausters of colour
Nature waits with the last playing card
We all take part in debarking

the last tree The last living I am there
Standing on a mountain and seeing everything
My stars Why did I stay?

Nature and man
Play the cards:
Gentlemen No trump! None!

Pictures in Motion

1

There's a little girl
sitting on a bar
of white marble
having no idea that it is part
of one of the hundreds of thousands
of cold crosses
which will be planted later
in the fields
when it has become quiet
And has no idea
why
but still smiles
and can't wait for Mom to come
and has no idea
that she will not come at all
and the sun warms a little
tries to bake on the smooth stone
but not enough for the girl
to keep on
smiling
And she rises carefully
and feels the tears
tickle her cheek
and she sees the light
Hears people walk by
Does not understand
that it is only
a picture
And no one ever
tells her

2

An officer stands in the middle
with a map on a table
He instructs He talks
about the next important step
And all the soldiers lie wounded
in an oval around him
and try to listen
But the blood in their ears
will not
and the officer looks around
he understands quite well
the lay of the land
and yet he asks the soldiers
how they feel
and they want to answer
but cannot
and the officer takes it easy
He has done this before
It will soon be over
It is only some kind of dream
he says
And something
hangs low in the air
above them
and is at the same time gone
for the last time
and there is no one
to tell them
that it is not
a dream

3

This is one of the pictures
one constantly feels a desire
to break into
Not to live there
but to save
all the little obscure
stooping carcasses
appearing to drift
endlessly from place to place
without achieving anything else
than being
silent elements
in a large composition
With their animals
which they drive
with naïve hands
without moving a single step
forward
One of the pictures
that you scream into
to save these lonely beings
from eternal immobility
But where they for a moment
turn around
and with their gray
squinted eyes
call me a Murderer
and return unhappily
to a life underneath the varnish
that no one understands

4

This staggering
between despair
and hope
This alternate
between silence
and screams
Between light
and emptiness between
stars
I imagine
us falling
while grabbing
words in the air
Up under the wings
that are
growing out
Their bright shiny
surfaces
Still wet
after the birth
still cautiously
hovering in the air
and later
when there is
no air:
During travels
pulled by the force
between stars
That is why we stagger
That is why we win in the end

5

We only move because
we feel the light Feel that
it touches us with its
cold and its warmth Because we
see colours shoving
us and getting us started
Only because we don´t have anything
to do here and have goals
that are distant to the eye but
near when we close it
and listen to the suction sounds of the road
The goal is the stars The goal
is for us to be able to touch
each other without creepy
evasions Without sweaty tremors
And as we move
we move everything else and
gain enemies who believe
we want them dead Who
will not believe that we are their
rescue and hide in
pictures without knowing
the colours and the shifts
in their flat grey world
But we still reach out
towards them and let them
hear our songs And when they
finally join us
the pictures will become alive to them too
and suddenly we have come much further

Travels in Sorrow

April's Fools

The gaping torsos of the alley
stand in the cold wind of peace
still with spring's longing for leaves
in the struggling cells

Once the trees were a part of life
and until they become so again
there is every reason to believe in the sun
and follow its slowly ascending path …

I am writing you a quiet letter
while a dog fills the street with its barking:
There are so many words I must fit
with your mouth and your eyes, your movements …

A dog, a letter; everything has an inner
unbearable connection
that one must acknowledge
when moving in the sprouting spring of the city:

The jesters dance into the month
with their blind faith in laughter
while we all know that the real jesters
will have a hard time under the kingdom of the sun!

Transit

A grieving woman
walks through the city

I have never seen
a city this white
a sky this blue
a sorrow this black

And yet
I can't hear her
I only see the water
Only the ship far away
that did not see us …

A grieving woman
walks through the city
whose houses are
empty shells
where cries of distress resound
in unanswered spirals

The trees are quiet
The wind is gone
I ask a bird
Why I should live
and it falls to the ground:
Was not prepared …

Notion Downfall

A plum falls softly
  almost inaudibly in the dark
    almost invisibly
      almost the same colour as the night

Numerous lives are lived
  in this downfall
    in the gravitation towards the centre
      in the relentless speed of gravity

And yet there are too many cells
  in this ripe fruit ready to travel
    to count them in time
      before the garden´s green skin is hit

But there is time to ask
  wherein the necessity lies
    of remembering and writing down
      this ultra-swift infinity

Again and again
  and again
    and again
      and again …

Even Though You Are Dead

Even though you are dead now
you are far too alive
for me to forget you

and I know
that you are not really dead
But rather, I am dead
to you

I also hope
that you feel more alive
than I do

For when the sun rises
the city becomes black to me
Clouds resemble
your many faces
and I must hide
in screaming stairwells
to not destroy
the days of everyone else

View

Stacks of books
that I should have read …
Little white notes everywhere
like shipwrecked vessels
from an unknown world:
All these words and views
I so carefully try not to forget
The flower in the flowerpot
which I gaze at, again and again:
The leaves have paled
pale yellow, pale green …
It must not die as well!
It is so important
Perhaps way too important

I have read the letters
What should I answer?
I will only be able to say:
"Yes, that's how it is!"
But I would rather
look through and beyond it all
At life outside
that continues pointlessly
remotely and silent
because the image of you
and your smile
will not disappear
and will not give
significance
to anything else

Signs of Spring

One sudden spring morning
there are seven sparrows in a tree
like a comforting sign …

As the day passes by
I follow their eyes
because I haven't seen yours
in such a long time

When the sun sets
the birds are gone
But the tree remains
like an abandoned skeleton
of an impossible dream

Inside a Mountain

Deep inside a mountain
there are no eyes
stealing time

Here it is as if
time stands still
because it can be longer
between the waterdrops in the cavities
than a life …

Here silence
is an oppressive constraint
you never get used to
but can't run away from
and no conversations
to break it
other than the stubborn
reproduction of the isotopes

Here beauty
isn't visible but present
in the dark of the crystals
Here jealousy
isn't a hurting reality
but a temporarily locked
game between elements

Deep inside a mountain
I am nothing

but a guess
an opportunity

Deep inside a mountain
there is no waiting time
nothing to reach or achieve
nothing to be too late for

Deep inside a mountain
no love is abandoned
Deep inside a mountain
I remember us lying close together
hugging each other even closer
to feel safe
when we woke up from time to time
in the endless course of the night …

There time was
an applied notion
You see it clearly here
deep inside a mountain
where there are no other sounds
than animal screaming from scattered caves

Here are hidden possible answers
to the coherence of occurrences:
You enter
and everything comes to a standstill

If you ever escape
everything will have changed anyhow

From the Dawn of Ages

Perhaps I awaken one morning
after this dreadful sleep

Perhaps I then find myself
in an entirely different place

where I will drink the time of morning
out of blue cups

Perhaps I will then see you
in the curious reflection of water

The Boy and the Sea

A little boy
drawing images in the sand

The sea rolls in
across the beach

As time throws itself
upon life

And before the boy
has removed the sand from his fingers

He is old and tired
and filled with dense images

Human Tracks

The land lies as long fibres
Through the swells of time
With its tracks in exposed places
after humans' hurtful axe strokes
humans' arson
humans' poisonings …

The air is thin like sharp paper
The sounds reproduce themselves across the land
in the deadly cable currents
and roads, waterways, escape routes …
Bleeding gashes and scratches
and slow animal migrations across the fields …

Everywhere there are houses
Sometimes someone moves
between an empty church and a dense forest
or between the beds of forgotten lovers
and the loss of one's only true love:
A movement which is without end …

And therefore also a land full of sorrow
and a land full of mourners
I have measured the distance again and again
between these houses in order to comprehend
the magnitude of their sorrow and measure it
against mine which does not appear to be any less …

Dancing Under the Gallows

The Picture

The picture of you radiates
an immense, embracing warmth
Our paths once crossed:
Our traces of back ends and loose ends
What did we think we would see
there in the imaginary light
What were the words
we heard each other forget?
We never really sensed;
our bodies
their contours silenced
by voices of infatuation
Now only remains the picture I drew;
clear lines
shielded behind your hidden dreams
Now I only wait for a single answer
That can set everything right:
One day you will be a scream
A light that cuts
straight through our shared paths
You will be a beacon to travel towards
What we never lost completely
and never could share

There Are Days

There are days when diseases
sweep across the land
Where inflammation attaches itself
to the forgotten crevices of the brains
and draws yellow traces of death
Days where diseases sneak in
on the slow-moving cattle herds
leaving us to dig holes in the night;
giant craters in the silent soil
These are the same days
where my inkwell tips over in the storm
Where the paper lies empty and screaming:
a white, neglected Siberia
with big blobs and lakes
absorbing and absorbing
and making me heavy with sluggish thoughts
Those are the days where I head out
in disregard of the morning´s promises,
disentangle the city's web of fear
and thinking that
perhaps you should cross one of the tracks
that I leave in this lonely night

It Can Be a Letter

It can be a letter
from you that makes me tremble
and feel obvious signs of fever;
an early, sudden typhoid of words
It can be one of the letters
that destroys an entire day
making the next days look like
random lasers of time
That´s when you write
that you can´t forget me
just like that
but would wish for both of us
that you could
and that is how you make sure to
stand in the way for both of us
and for everything to be dragged out
to unrecognisable yearnings

Big Heavy Birds

Big heavy birds
fly away with our houses
Insects' eyes follow the city´s movements
on this special day
Soon the world is ready
for new upheavals
of light and screaming
In these final ears
Music is heard about time:
The globe on the big voyage
The mind packed with fear
and thoughts about what will happen
The day darkens under the beat of the wings
Soon it will be a new day
Soon the silence will crack
Soon we are back

Now Hangs the Foggy Seal of the Moon

Now hangs the foggy seal of the moon
and laughs behind the bars of winter trees
Now owl tongues light up
in the white lights of thoughts …
It is the ice age now
and someone screams
a final word
about what we didn´t get to do
It is departure times,
human ending
closing of eyes and countries
It is hope being frozen
to small knots
of frost and despair …

Wake Up

Wake up you winter souls
And speak up, for there are listeners
To all words that shine brightly
Jump from your ridges
On the cold cliff, in the whistling of the air:
Sprouting is hidden in the sleep
There is caress and movement
under the thin crust of frost
there is warmth and touching
in a time that comes
– if we want!
Out of the frost the day breaks
it is bright with hope and eyes
A world without inner wounds of threats
and full of joyful faces
A flower of life unfolds proud leaves
that cover time and extinguish darkness
and give life to dreams!

There Is Always an Opening

There is always an opening in the choir
for outbreaks of scattered voices
Therefore I will sing the lead
to images of an early age
They are filled with heavy birds
Black, silent bodies hovering
They know even more than us
about the dangers of these landscapes
Because they are full of ruins
Churches abandoned by the last congregation
although an individual, monk or dreamer,
can get lost in there in a quiet winter
Their open, slim windows
look like angels with their crying heads turned
Here they remain for some time around a cross
no conversation, no eyes, no time
Between two pages in this book
I find a strand of hair white from curved age
as an impatient sign from someone deceased
or from a sudden present future ...
On these pages the ice packs itself across
the screeching hull of a ship
A storm has left this place
taking waves of screams and frost with it
But there are often lovers
in these mountains where the fog boils
a quivering in our limbs when my love
reaches for a sign, a cairn
on routes between these demonic images

A lover's couple, all all alone
in an orange whisper, over a dark blue deep
Lovers reaching out for each other
and after a sure sign of movement
as the movement can be a measly cabin
sheltered by ruins yearning for the sky
or the wavy migration of a herd of sheep
We are like gaping spectators;
quivering parents holding our children
back at the entrance of a graveyard
in such decay that it can only be
a painting: But the smells are there and
the sounds When the sounds are there it is
rumbling and banging, a squealing of nature
Otherwise everything is silent as a rainbow
And we are not just The Viewers
but trapped in a painful privity
of these orbiting birds:
So heavy from fear and happiness

As for Love

As for love
between the two of us
I must seek help
in a deep, heartfelt memory
Of our silent touches
Our eyes portrayed happiness
clearly, evidently …
Careful smiles sealing
The Great Love
we never dreamt
could wither
And yet …
I no longer feel
your reassuring traces
on my body
but remember them clearly
as an incredible
scathing shiver
In a way
Our bodies are still one
The same Zodiac signs
tie us together
wherever we go
However often our lonely paths
happen to cross
we fill out
the same net
of actions
the same words

as if we were still
united, sanctified
to this recollected joy
We always loved searchingly
Everything was so unknown and so big
as soon as the days piled up
around our private signs
Yes, the days
They were the ones intruding
pushing in between us
because we shared them in the wrong way
on our journey towards
the Land of the Adults
We let them slip away
We let each other go
Because we knew nothing
That is why we still love
also in this detached time
where we must talk
with mountains of doubt
and bewildered storms
between us
but with the same words
as if we were still …

A Poem

A poem
written on your shoulder blade
one late evening
So beautiful
your obliging skin
So happily
it flew away
the perishable paper
leaving the lives of the words
in our hands

Ice Age, Ice Dream

Ice age, ice dream
you give me warm yearnings
When I catch a glimpse of you
I think of the countries in the South
that we travelled through, silently
in each other's hands
These deep, green lungs …
How often the gardens have
opened to us,
rivers flown to our words
that were often saturated by silence
I think they will do it again
Magnolias bloom
Big white flakes
On the summer sky
Somewhere distant we walk
you and I
It can never end

Near the Distance

Of the Same Dreams

There across the ocean
Lies the other coast
The distant land
That I long for

Just like the flying fish long
To hover
Above the ship masts
And subdue two elements

Just like the dolphins long
To tell humans
Their wise peculiar stories
Of happiness and the balance of nature

The land we saw
When we were two to see
And two to wake up
From the same dreams.

Life and Death From Above

From the mountain
Flows the water
Beneath the mountain
Known by all
Lies the city
Lives and drinks

From the mountain
Flows the lava
Jolts the fire
Under the ashes
Lies the city
Forgotten by all.

Departure

I stand in a city
Where the streets are so narrow
That it has been abandoned by cars

I penetrate its veins
Where the alleys threaten to swallow me
In their dense, entangled tissue

I hide
Where a road ends and a house begins
Because I know I must leave today

I am in a city I have missed so often
As the only body
That can accommodate my mind

I leave and arrive
From and to the same courteous house
The same distressed landscape

Neither to nor from 'happiness'
The pain and longing
We call the journey´s destination.

South of My Heart

You have travelled to an island
South of my heart
The same moon
Shines for us
Here north of your doubt
So distant from your glance

You have travelled to an island
On wings of uncertainty
Left alone with the dream
I think of you
Ravaged by your absence
When you return
Have you really returned then
Or are you now an island yourself
Where I shall never be stranded
Painful as the sea
Abandoned by the waves
The body whose blood
Has been washed away
Awaiting and empty
Am I in your nights
A flap of the dreams
You struggle against
Do you love me
As I adore you
Or are you nothing but a stranger

On this remote island
South of my heart
In the centre of my mind
Are you the one I think you are
As of yet
I am the same
Yours for a life
If you want
Come back
And let me come
Really home.

Celebration for a Saint

Did my laundry this morning
In the cool light of the basement
While the sun bathed the town above the valley
A brass band played out of tune
Facing the church
And cannons thundered
In an entirely different age

Hung the clothes out to dry
On the windblown roof
With clothes pins as big as swallows
And the fog crept down from the mountain
I saw it myself
Like a gray silent army
Ready to take over the village above the valley

And the clothes kept hanging
As the night fell
Fireworks were in the air
With star glimpses and luminous smoke
And entire crusades passed through the streets
So that no one saw or heard
The wings that flew away with my clothes.

The Man With the White Hat

The man with the white hat
Folds the sun loungers
And stacks them in colourful piles

With bare feet
He evens out the sandcastles
Gently as the rhythm of the waves

With his distant dark eyes
He watches the coins glistening in his bag
And the day fading to nothing.

As You Once Were

Somewhere I saw you
As you once were

Where a cliff crept forward
As an animal born by the sea

You sat surrounded by waves
Confined in the distance of time

On a rock almost an island
Scouting towards the land of the dolphins.

The Tea Leaf Pickers

The yellow-blue swarms over the tea fields
The soft sound of leaves being picked
Soundless is the sky above the tea leaf pickers
And in the night their hands
Are silent as stars.

The Sea of Change

The Anatomy of Melancholy

In this garden I must linger
For as long as it takes it to become
A desert an ocean a forest and a garden again
And it must be one single movement
To be here amidst all the ships
Proudly passing with the serenity of swans
The place where I sat down
For a moment to listen to the water
And the wind brushing the leaves
In the same way that I wish
To greet time in this moment
Where the sky is eternity itself
And I feel joy because the sun
Is warm and bright and I have nothing
To escape from except my lingering
In this garden where I remain
For just as long as I want to or can
Until my inner turmoil flares up
Where I would die if I could not
Get up and leave
This garden with melancholy and an urge to travel
So full of the birds' security
Exhilarated by the calling of the horizon
In other gardens I will linger
And retain the love
I always seek to
Maintain in this the only way possible

In All These Images

In all these images
I am transformed
In one of them you enter
Our child is born
And time shimmers in the light
Like falling leaves

The Moment

Live in the present
You are your own extent of time
Time follows you
The past is lost
And the future you will never have

But you have these dandelions
Which brighten the room
And your daughter's seconds
Of bliss and progress
For one moment

The Fisherman

Every day
Since he was born
On an ancient coast
He has seen the sea
Like a silver tray
As the evening nears

The sun being cleaved
Like a luminous orange
By a mountain peak
While the storks fly away
And the fish surface
To kiss goodnight

Every single night
He has dreamt
About those images
While the moon sang silence
And the trees whispered
In darkness about the world

Every year he has lived
To pass on
These images
To have someone
With whom to share
These infinite moments

The Sea of Dreams

1

The sea has caught fire
Floating gold washing up on the beach
The sunshades stretching to cover this miracle
The best they can

Soon the sun will disappear in the waves
The fire will die out
And the gold will be found
In the dreams of thousands

2

The sea gnawing at the coast
Sand tumbling down the cliff
Encapsulated time atomised
Petrifaction broken

A glimpse of eternity
So short
That all I have time to say
Is

I'm here

Reborn

1

I have hidden in a desert
To forget the sea

But the wind sounds like the sea
And washes away my security

Small grains of pain
Flow through my memory

Just before the next silence
The next reunion with light

2

I swim in black waves
All night they have hidden the darkness

Unseen I walk unto the shore
And feel as light as moonlight

In this light the sandcastles vanish
And with them all failed beginnings

Yesterday I was a child last night a fish
Today some tracks on a beach

The Lying Tree

First they called him
The wandering hourglass
Because you could almost see
Life leaving his body
And transforming his body
To a withered swaying stalk

The day he no longer
Moved among them
They respectfully called him
The lying tree
And all the birds came
And sat on him

They followed his breath
With their wingbeat
And never even left him
The day the earth laid down
Over their plumage
And turned day to night

I Caress the Wind

I caress the wind
Because it is the closest
I can get to your cheek

I plant a tree
To understand
Something without us

Dragon Valley

In this valley
Where dragons and monsters
Once ate grown-ups and children
The rain now pours
In a rainforest darkness
As evening falls

Thunder roars
And is thrown from side to side
Between the rock walls
Some deer stand as petrified
Inherited dragon fear
Still in their eyes

While lightning strikes
In the treetops
And our small human family
Walk in a single file
Across flimsy suspension bridges
And rushing streams

At the end of the valley
We find our car
Surrounded by peacocks
Pleased that the dust
Has finally been washed away
After months of drought

Relieved that all went well
We drive home across the mountains
And see a pillar of fire
Appear behind us
As a farewell greeting
From the awakening caves of the night

One Who Resembled You

I saw someone who resembled you
Walk with someone who resembled me,
But they were not us
And so I cried again

The sea pained me
When I tried to see it again
For what is the sea without you
What is any land without you

And so I am stranded again
On this shore where there are no ships
To take me away
And the cliff is too high to overcome

But today summer arrived regardless
So suddenly that it skipped spring
And with the sunny beginning
I feel hope and trust blossom again

Moon, See Me

Come up to me, trees
Through the grass that absorbs the rain
Come and grow
In that instant which is my life

Climb down to me, sky
Seize me with stars
With your endless, wet night
And calming sapphire sea

See me, moon, at the frontier
Of my ultimate love
I reflect myself in you
And to my pleasure
I see the face of my beloved

Everything Is an Opening

See, the Little Boy Is Playing

See, the little boy is playing
The small green tanks roll forward
Under his innocent hands
The sounds from his mouth
Are the language of the infinite land of imagination

See, his hands are dark clouds
His play is a challenge of death
He dreams and wonders
Plays out all that
He knows must never happen

See, from his hands the rain falls
The small green tanks come to a stop
He will soon be in bed
Dreaming about angels
And wars that cannot be undone.

Father

Then you disappeared
Into the mists of powerlessness

Your son withdrew
Into the wilderness of continuity

Two little boys
In the undergrowth of imagination

Maybe they will meet
In a clearing of forgiveness

Maybe they will each find
Their own path towards the explanation

But there is no way back
Over the images' walls of pain

There is only onward, forward
Towards the place where the past subsides

Where the present fills everything and
Forgiveness is an unconscious act.

The Evening People

There they are, the evening people
Trying to predict the trajectory of the sun
And wish for it to never set

They do not sit until they think
They know where the light will touch at the end

There they are, deliberating, dreaming
And they won't wake up until the shadows
Melt together.

My Daughter

My daughter comes running to me
Completely still I wait
For her to be born again
Before my humble glance

I pray that my heart
Will meet her fully open
Not because she is my daughter
But because I am the mirror of her trust.

The Clock in the Telephone

I am on the phone
With my ex-wife
Just a moment, please
Says her voice
A clock is ticking
Somewhere at the other end

A clock is ticking and time passes
I hear my daughter singing
Somewhere at the other end
So close to my heart
So far from my touch
A clock is ticking and time passes

Several photo albums pass by
They smack like machine guns firing
For every album, a chapter of life closes
And falls into the archives of the mind
So close to my ear
So distant from this life

Time passes, time passes
The food was burning
Says the voice of my ex-wife
Oh, just that, I answer
While the whizz of perplexity
Crawls into my ear

So far from my reality
Take care, talk to you soon
I say while the clock is ticking
Somewhere at the other end
As a metronome to the tune of
The restless pulse of my blood

My daughter's song
Clicks into a well-known signal
Escaping through endless poppy fields
Through cutting flames of globes
And starry eyes of frozen rivers;
Signifying closure.

Full Moon

Full moon
Face
A life
Opens
And lights up
Comes
Towards an encounter

The face of
My child
A greeting
As the sky
Is bright
A kiss
Before night.

Fishermen

We are sailing
My daughter and I
On the turbulent ocean
The mountains are the bodies of ancient times
The ocean is infinite
We look towards the sun
That never sets

We fish
My daughter and I
Upon unfamiliar waves
Below us silver bodies slide by
We pull and let go
Pull and let go
Keeping bait and hook in constant motion

We hope
My daughter and I
For the great catch
For resistance from the line
The first jerk in the rod
When a fish bites the bait
Betrayed by the deadly metal fish

We win
My daughter and I
We both catch our very first fish
Our eyes sparkle, we cut up the fish
Each sitting with our own
Tiny beating fish heart
In our bloody hands.

Message in a Bottle

We toss our message in a bottle
Into the white foam on the black sea
A seven-year-old girl's letter to the world

My soon-to-be big daughter lifted up
In my arms at the stern of the ship
So frighteningly near the abyss of life

She clings to me with her suntanned arms
Her dress flutters in the cool wind
Anxious eyes and an anticipating smile

Now the bottle flies over the foam
Sailing on the waves before disappearing behind us
In the darkness towards the kingdom of the sea people

Do you think they will remember to write me?
She asks with hope in her tiny voice
Someday there might be an answer, I say

Our voices are drowned by the roaring night
Soon we are sound asleep in the bunk bed below deck
Just like the letter coiled up in the bottle

It has been a year now and no one has answered
Perhaps the bottle found a crack in the cliffs
Where it waits for a finder from another time

Perhaps it is still travelling the seas
The small plastic bottle with a drawing of a ship
Greetings from a girl growing older

Second by second the signal is coming
Through time that stops or is still in motion
Until met by someone who waited

I hope for an answer while we are here together
An answer confirming that it does make sense to ask
I want to see my daughter's eyes when the answer arrives.

Dad, Is This a Dream

Dad, is this a dream
Or is it real
Squeeze my hand

Tell me, dad
Did you dream me
Before I was born

Would you also want me
Dad, if you knew
I wasn't me

Do you know, Dad
How lucky you are
That it was me you had?

Dad, is this a dream
Or is it real
Squeeze my hand.

Angel Child

You light a candle
My child
In this church
So sweet and tiny
As if it was built
For you

Before the eyes of all the icons
We put money in the collection box
And I snap a picture of you
My child, in your baby blue dress
While you light a candle
And your angel eyes shine.

Across All Deserts

I must travel
Across all deserts
To get sand for
You my daughter

I must climb
Mountains through the snow
And torn cliffs
In fever-thin air

I must swim
Across the ocean
As vast as
All my love

I must clean up
And clear the road
So we can rediscover
The world together.

I See You

Sometime
Will be the last time
That I see you

The thought is unbearable especially now
That you disappear behind a house
To play with other carefree children

Sometime
Will be the last time
That I see you, the sun, the sky

Will you be a child then or a grown-up?
Will I still be young or old?
And will I know when it happens?

Or maybe no time
Is quite the last time
Maybe there will always be a reunion

Maybe every death
Every birth
Is a reunion

I see you
The sun, the sky
Again.

Between To and From

I love the waiting time
Wherein space opens
The clockwork system succumbs
To the searching pulse of the body

In the waiting time I'm left
To myself and to the order of the universe
I wait in a train to arrive
Enriched by the vacuum between two points

I catch myself hoping
That I will never really arrive
That the plane will remain in the sun above the clouds
Until I fill out space completely

Between to and from
Between you and nothing
Between arms that open
And the child that runs to me shining.

Everything Is an Opening

There is a place
Where everything is an opening
Where the membrane of darkness cracks
And light penetrates everything

Where the clammed-up mussel
Is an opening towards itself
Because there is more inside of it
Than in everything outside

There is a place
Where the stone opens inwards
And seen from its interior is transparent
Because it contains everything.

The Last Lovers

I float above the bed
And watch us make love

Everything is transparent

Your movements are
Like an infinite birth

Were we the last lovers?

It has been long since
We made love for the last time

All has ended

Everything is the same
The picture flickers into view.

New poems

Dark Time

Have just seen the moon
Move, move me
while the wing of a bat
brushed my head
and created a surge
in my coffee cup

We approach the future:
It waits impatiently
on the other side of the night
as it slowly
darkens and the pulse
becomes clearer:
The sound of the heart
while the stars
compose lullabies
on the music notes of the aerials

There is a special rhythm in silence
whilst the night subtly
sneaks forward
and prevents me
from seeing what I
have written …

Black and White

Even in the middle of the night
the room is white,
its walls glowing
to compete with the stillness
which is enhanced by
the silence of the dead flies

I get up
and walk to the window,
open it
and blow the flies
from the windowsill
out into the moonlight

One last time
they fly,
and as they settle
they colour
the snow
black.

Home With the Nation

Suddenly one morning
the room is empty

The lit-up window square
stares emptily from the dark façade
as a misprinted stamp
confused about its lost identity

Someone died
Someone gets a new life
Someone grieves
Someone rejoices

There is something ruthless
about a day like this
that pretends
that everything is as usual
that everything will go back to what it was

As if a room
can feel abandoned one morning
when it is still dark
and everyone
almost everyone
is on their way.

Winterland

Every night I go to bed early
in the hope that sleep will erase
all traces of the day's wanderings,
after the river of dark thoughts
flooding my mind
sending my thoughts
on an endless ferry crossing
from shore to shore

Every night I go to bed early
in the hope that my dreams
will let me into
edifying landscapes
and flush away the sorrow

Every night I go to bed early
in the hope that the night will absorb the grief,
the intangible, homeless grief
the coming-from-nowhere,
the unwanted, irrational grief
that the distinctive music of the night
will dissolve the patterns of the shadows

Every morning I awaken
and walk into the
all-consuming labyrinths
of everyday life,
sailing on the human sea of the city
and looking for a way out.

The Red Balloon

The biggest dream
has become a stone

A dull termination
Sent from outer space

We leave meaningless days behind us,
Try to remember love

In time it all disappears,
even the voices and the sky

That is why we are here.

On the Other Side of the Ocean

On the other side of the ocean
I see the town clinging to the cliff,
white and bright, highly elevated beyond time

Above the large seaside hotel
where my mother stayed with her parents
one summer more than 80 years ago

With my binoculars I see her,
the little girl in her flowery dress,
laughing happily on the balcony

She sees me and waves
and knows I am on my way
somewhere out there in her future.

Lose Grip

I am building a house of words for you
You enter, and the walls tumble,
but the words rise.

From the roots the words grow
through you,
their fibres become part of you.

Your foundation disappears,
you lose grip
you fall,
       fall,
           fall …

But the words seize you,
you grasp them,
it is no longer you and me.

Nothing is out or in,
no longer a place,
but movement.

Because you entered through
the entrance I wrote,
we have both moved.

Together we have overturned the world
and won it. Ready
for new openings. Stronger.

I no longer know,
where I am,
Only that you are here.

The words are no longer mine,
but ours. The words and us,
never quite the same.

The new world is yours.

Reflection

In a window
Up high in the hospital
A person stands
diluted by the light
– at the edge of life

From each our side of the world
we both see the Moon
hanging like a luminous yoyo
Frozen in time between our dreams
As distant and as close as a stranger

Our gazes join
The Moon holds us
and moves us
We don't know who we see
when we look at our reflection

Only that
we meet
in one way
or another.

Nothing

Nothing lasts
forever

But
the tireless
growing pains
of the Universe.

Notes

The poems in this selection appear in the same order as in the original poetry collections.

Translation from Danish to English by Anne-Mette Damon.

Except:

'The Anatomy of Melancholy', 'The Fisherman', 'The Tea Leaf Pickers' by Nena Sue Thomassen.

'Moon, See Me', 'One Who Resembled You', 'The Last Lovers' by Sheema Kalbasi.

'I Caress the Wind', 'Reborn' by John Mason.

Poetry collections by Jens Fink-Jensen

Original Danish title and year of publication:

World in an Eye: *Verden i et øje,* 1981

Travels in Sorrow: *Sorgrejser,* 1982

Dancing Under the Gallows: *Dans under galgen,* 1983

Near the Distance: *Nær afstanden,* 1988

The Sea of Change: *Forvandlingshavet,* 1995

Everything is an Opening: *Alt er en åbning,* 2002

The Sea of Change

The English translation of 'The Anatomy of Melancholy' was first published in the anthology of the 4th International Literary Festival, Nicosia, Cyprus, in 2019.

New poems

The poems are written between 2003 and 2022.

'Winterland', 'The Red Balloon', and 'On the Other Side of the Ocean' were first published in the literary magazine *Victor B. Andersens Maskinfabrik,* no. 64, Copenhagen, April 2018. 'Lose Grip' was first published in the programme for the Copenhagen Literature Festival – KBH Læser – in 2018.